This book belongs to:

FOX

TEASERS
TWISTERS
STUMPERS

a bookful of tricky Torah-riddles

by Yaffa Ganz

design/illustration: Harvey Klineman

Teaser, Twister and Stumper answers are on the last page of the book

First published 1989
Copyright © 1989 by Yaffa Ganz

Philipp Feldheim Inc.
200 Airport Executive Park
Spring Valley, NY 10977

Feldheim Publishers Ltd.
POB 6525 / Jerusalem, Israel

Library of Congress Cataloging-in-Publication Data

Ganz, Yaffa
Twisters, teasers, stumpers : a bookful of tricky Torah riddles /
by Yaffa Ganz.
p. cm.
Summary: A collection of riddles based on the Torah and Jewish topics
ISBN 0-87306-517-4 (U.S.)
1. Judaism—Juvenile literature.   2. Riddles, Juvenile.
[1. Judaism—Wit and humor.   2. Riddles.] I. Title.
BM573.G37   1989   89-23623
296'.0207--dc20   CIP
                                                                    AC

Printed in Israel

for Gershon Achiya נ״י
great-grandson of
Gershon ben Shaul Halevi ז״ל

Easier
Teasers

1

I'm not a clock –
but I tell time
The day, the month,
the year.
I mark each week,
and Shabbos too,
In boxes bright and clear.
Looking for a holiday?
I'll tell you if it's near.
  What am I?

It hops, it skips, it jumps.
It's damp and full of lumps.
It filled the land of Egypt
With awful groans and grumps.

What was it?

3 We're hot at the top
And we soon disappear.
You can't start a Yom Tov
Unless we are here.

Sometimes we're colored.
Sometimes we're white.
We start with a Nun;
We'll make your room bright.

WHAT

ARE

WE ?

4

I'm crunchy and thin
And not at all fine.
Each year you will eat me
With eggs, herbs and wine.
The Jews rush to make me,
No waiting till later.
Perhaps you will bake me
To eat at your seder.

What am I?

I hurled a smooth stone
Through the air at his head.
With a whopping crash
   and clatter,
The evil giant fell dead.

Who am I and who was he?

6

Rachel slept on yellow straw,
Her house was poor and bare.
But yellow-gold was her reward
To wear upon her hair.

Who was she and why
was she rewarded?

7

I can look fat
or tall or thin.
It all depends
Whether you
spill me out,
Or pour me in.
I'm red or purple,
sour or sweet.
At certain times,
you may not eat
Until a bracha
(just for me!)
Is heard by all
the family.

What am I ???

In winter snow, in ice and cold
I'll bring you back to days of old.
You'll watch me turn and dance around
Though I've no feet to touch the ground.
The letters that I own are four.
They tell of wondrous things galore.

What am I?

We're fresh, soft, and shiny
When you bring us home.
Our braids are just perfect,
Although we've no comb.

Two friends, fat and chummy
We've got quite a tan.
You might say we're crummy.
We met in a pan.

What are we?

Once we spoke;
you listened to me.
But now I am the enemy.
I planned, connived,
your life to steal;
Watch out or I might
bite your heel!

What am I?

11 "Don't stop! Don't turn!"
Her hearing's faulty.
And that is why
She turned so salty.
Who is she?

What am I?
Do you know me?
I blow a choppy melody.
I'm hard as rocks
and stiff as bones.
I sing a song with
just three tones.
You'll hear my call
and certainly try
To be good or better.
I'll tell you why.
I help remind you
not to sin.
My name starts with
the letter shin.

What am I?

I'm thin and white
And filled with black,
And if I ever tear or crack
You'll fix me up quick-as-can-be
And put me back for all to see.
I'm never on a wall or floor.
My place is always near the door.
I don't stand straight, I'm rolled up tight.
I guard your home by day and night.

What am I?

Round and bumpy, full of seeds,
Filled with juicy rows of beads.
Halfway sour, halfway sweet,
Shiny, moist and good to eat.
Hard and leathery is my rind,
Fifth of seven special kinds.

15

I bet you wouldn't eat a shoe
Or find a scarf too tasty.
And if you tried to bite a book
The pages would seem pasty.
But once a year you eat my hat!
Why do you do a thing like that?
Some people eat my pockets too,
Or bite my ears and chew and chew.
Now who am I, and when do they
Act in such a funny way?

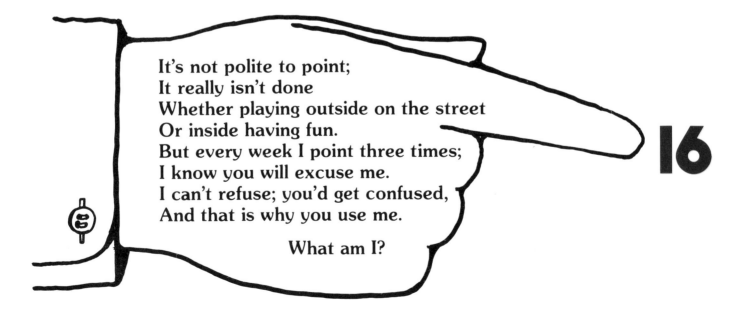

It's not polite to point;
It really isn't done
Whether playing outside on the street
Or inside having fun.
But every week I point three times;
I know you will excuse me.
I can't refuse; you'd get confused,
And that is why you use me.

What am I?

16

What am I? Do you know me?
I'm skinny and tall;
I grow on a tree.
I wave and I bend
With a round, lumpy friend.
You make a bracha on me.

What am I?

Down from the sky,
straight to the land
Covered and clean,
I lay on the sand.
Were Jews feeling hungry?
No need to cook!
They just opened their tents
And took a good look.
If they followed the rules,
Nothing would spoil.
They gathered me up
Without any toil.

What am I?

I'm proud and tall, I'm full of light.
I stand above my friends each night.
Although the blessing's not for me
I'm there to use, if not to see.

What am I?

It's awfully wet and damp outside.
We're lucky we can take this ride.
And even though we can't go out,
The man in charge here will provide.

Where are we?

Tougher Twisters

21

Loaded with camels,
jewels and spice
Off went a servant
to search for a wife.

Who was he?

23

"Down the rope
and through the window
Run away and save your life!"
Thus she spoke,
a kingly daughter
But not yet a kingly wife.

Who was she and
whom did she speak to?

22

*Someone sat and someone stood
And someone else stood too.
Someone's hands were held up high
Until the fight was through.*

*Who sat,
who stood,
and who fought
with whom?*

24

I swallow things, both round and flat
One at a time.
You take them out, all at once
Some other time.
It's a mitzva to fill me up
At any time,
Except for certain times
When it's the wrong time.

What am I?

25

As mountains go, I'm rather low
But even so, you surely know
My name, my house, my city.
And if you don't I sadly fear
You won't come up three times a year
And that would be a pity!

What's my name, my house, my city?

26

Drink, smell, see!
Whatever can I be?
I'm only here
To go away.
You say goodbye with me.

What am I?

27

I was played by a lad
To end a king's cries.
I was played by the wind
To make a king rise.
I was played by a king
Who sang songs of praise.
Too bad you can't hear
My tune nowadays.

What am I?

28

He planted a tree and set up a tent.
He gave food for free and didn't charge rent.

Who was he and where was his tree?

She sat upon her camel
Refusing to alight,
While her father searched and threatened,
While her father picked a fight.
She spirited away the spirits he did crave.
But she didn't share her secret
And it led her to the grave.

Who was she and what were the "spirits"?

Floating in the reedy water,
Packed in gopher wood and tar,
Discovered by a royal daughter,
Both will leave and travel far.

Can you name them both?

31
My master thought he was so smart.
He ordered me to move, to start.
But I wouldn't move; I wouldn't walk;
Although I *did* begin to talk.

What am I?

32

Up that ladder,
Pass that brick, please.
We are reaching to the sky.
Let's get going, We shall conquer
All the powers that rule on high.
With just one stroke their project ended.
No more building, no more pride.
And instead of climbing upwards,
They were scattered far and wide.

Who were they?

33
There's plenty to eat.
Take whatever you wish.
Every item's a treat.
Just avoid this one dish.

Where are you and what's the dish?

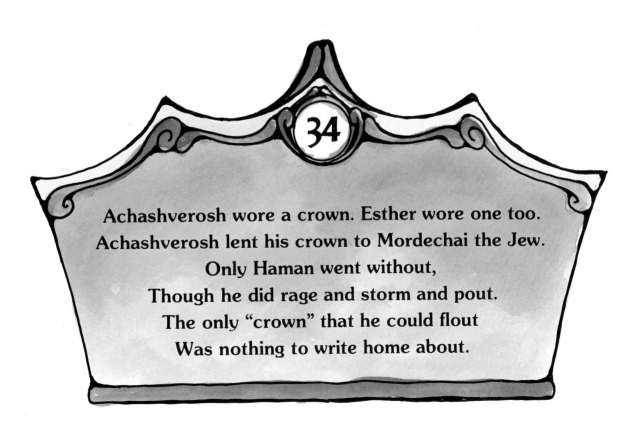

34

Achashverosh wore a crown. Esther wore one too.
Achashverosh lent his crown to Mordechai the Jew.
Only Haman went without,
Though he did rage and storm and pout.
The only "crown" that he could flout
Was nothing to write home about.

Who "crowned" Haman and how?

I'm curly or straight
And I always sit
on the sidelines —
Never in the center.
I grow down,
But not up.
The barber doesn't
scare me one bit.

What am I?

Silent stones
arranged in a square;
Silent stones which
only one could wear.
Silent stones
with a message clear;
Silent stones which
you could "hear".

Who wore them and
what were they?

I bleat and cry,
I'm all alone,
Afraid of the cat,
the fire, the stick.
I wish you'd come
And save me quick!

What am I?

Rooms have ceilings, windows, floors.
Yards have fences; houses doors.
Usually a wall is flat,
Standing still and that is that.
But this one wall got quite a start.
A few bouts of blowing
And it promptly fell apart.

What wall was this?

39

I don't come from a kosher creature
But you can eat me - ask your teacher!
I'm sticky and messy,
I won't make you thinner.
Yet two days a year
You'll invite me to dinner.

What am I?

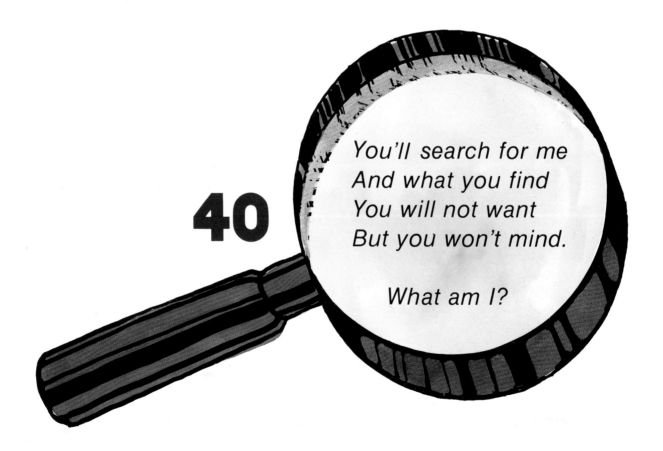

40

You'll search for me
And what you find
You will not want
But you won't mind.

What am I?

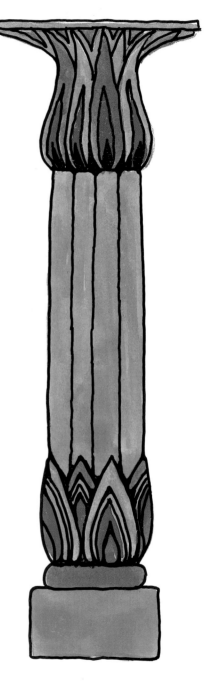

Who will find it? Where's it hidden?
Moshe searched both high and low.
Promises should not be broken.
Out of Egypt it must go.
"Hidden deep beneath the water!"
So said Serach, Asher's daughter.
Even Moshe could not lift it,
But he called and up it came.
After many years of waiting
It had answered to its name.
And for miles and years it travelled,
over rock and over sand,
Till it reached the proper country,
Till it reached the Promised Land.

what was it?

42

I crawled like a snake and split open seas
And made water flow from the funniest places.

What am I?

Three
little
letters
Declare a thing is true.
Three
little
letters
To know a thing is through.

What letters are they?

One prayed for a son
Because she had none.
And one who had many
Remained without any.
Both women of fame
Who shared the same name.

Who were they?

45

*I live on a square
With a hole
in the middle.
But I stick to
the corners and
add up to 613.*

What am I?

46 A word from the wise
is sufficient,
And the word you put in
did suffice.
In the blink of an eye
The villain did die
Because of your timely advice.

Who gave advice
to whom?

47

Five were the daughters
with one family name.
Five were the daughters;
great was their fame.
They appeared before Moses,
demanded and got
Their brother's share,
their father's lot.

Whose daughters were they
and what were their names?

48

A queen set to sea
in a sumptuous ship
Determined to see for
herself what was true.
Was the wise, famous king
more or less wise than she,
And once she had seen,
she sailed back with her crew.

Who was she
and whom
did she come
to see?

49

So royal a prince, so comely and fair!
Regal in bearing and proud of his hair.
But alas, his long locks did prove his ruin.
Their use was most inopportune.

Who was he?

50

He took nine-hundred chariots
And out he went to fight.
He lost nine-hundred chariots
To one whose name was bright.
A woman told him what to do.
Her "second" name gave light.

WHO lost the chariots?
won the fight?
was the woman?

51

Flax upon a roof and a hanging scarlet cord
Saved lives and gained a promise
To put away their sword.

Whose roof? Whose lives? What promise?

52

Four donkeys lost,
One kingdom found.
Who was annointed?
And who would be crowned?

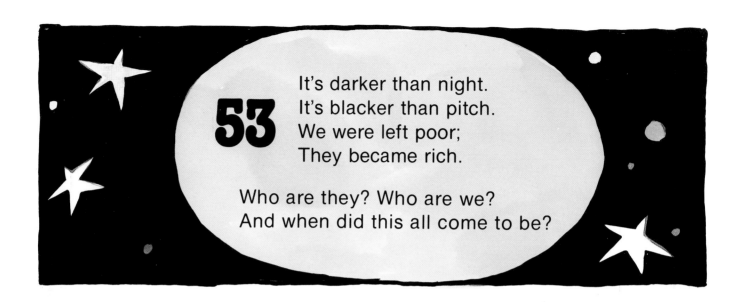

53
It's darker than night.
It's blacker than pitch.
We were left poor;
They became rich.

Who are they? Who are we?
And when did this all come to be?

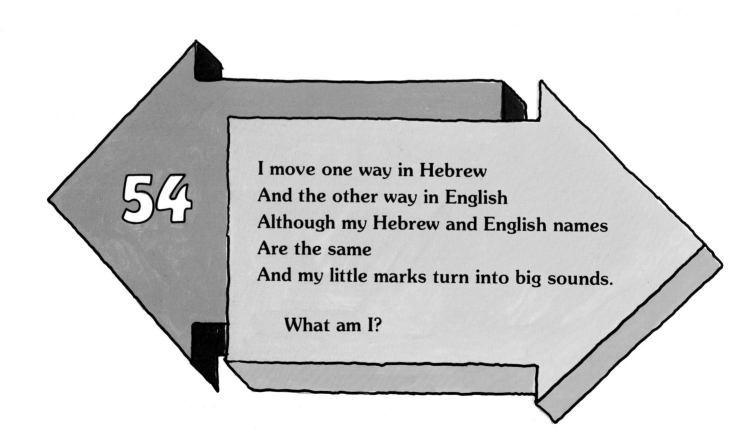

54
I move one way in Hebrew
And the other way in English
Although my Hebrew and English names
Are the same
And my little marks turn into big sounds.

What am I?

55

Swaying away
on my lonely string
I never learned
to dance or sing.
But once I spun
a crisscross ring
Of silky thread
to save a king.

Who or what am I?

56

Full of fire
I flew up high
Carrying someone
to the sky.
Despite the fire,
I did not burn.
He was not hurt.
He will return.

What am I
and who is he?

I am called double,
Although I hold eight.
I was paid for in full,
Although I was offered for free.
People come to see me,
Although I am deep in the ground
And am tightly sealed.

What and where am I?

Meeting at their special place
Where they would deliberate;
Three-score plus eleven strong,
They decided right from wrong.

Who were they?

59

Was it friend? Was it foe?
It fought through the night.
And though I was wounded
I still won the fight.

Who am I and who fought with me?

60

The time wasn't ripe,
The sun wouldn't set.
The moon wouldn't rise,
At least not yet.
They were fighting in a valley
And although they did not dally
They would need some time to rally
And overcome the threat.

What valley?
Who was fighting with whom?

MAZEL TOV!
You've reached the end.
Now turn the pages backwards
and you can start again!

Teasers

1. a calendar
2. The Second Plague — frogs
3. *nerot* — candles
4. matza
5. David; Goliath
6. Rabbi Akiva's wife; because she sent Akiva away for twenty-four years to learn Torah
7. wine
8. a Chanuka dreidel
9. two challas
10. the snake from Gan Eden
11. Lot's wife
12. a shofar
13. a mezuza
14. a pomegranate
15. Haman; on Purim, when they eat hamentashen
16. a Torah pointer
17. a lulav
18. manna
19. the *shamash* in the Chanuka menora
20. in Noah's ark

Twisters

21. Eliezer, the servant of Avraham
22. Moshe sat; Aharon and Chur stood; the Jews fought with Amalek
23. Michal, daughter of Shaul, spoke to David
24. a tzedaka box
25. Har Hamoriya; the Beit Hamikdash; Jerusalem
26. Havdala
27. David's harp
28. Avraham Avinu; in Beersheva
29. Rachel; Lavan's idols
30. Moshe and Bitya, Pharaoh's daughter
31. Bilaam's donkey
32. the builders of the Tower of Bavel
33. in Gan Eden; the fruit of the Tree of Knowledge
34. his daughter. She threw garbage on his head by mistake
35. peyot (sidelocks)
36. the Kohen Gadol (High Priest); the Urim VeTumim
37. Chad Gadya — The "One Kid" of the Hagadda
38. the wall around the city of Jericho
39. honey for Rosh Hashana
40. chametz

Stumpers

41. Yosef's coffin
42. Moshe's staff
43. AMeN = אמן
44. Chana, mother of Shemuel the Prophet; Chana, mother of seven sons killed by Antiochus
45. tzitzit
46. Charvona; to King Achashverosh
47. the daughters of Tzlafchad: Machla, Noa, Chogla, Milka and Tirza
48. the Queen of Sheba; Shlomo Hamelech
49. Avshalom, son of King David
50. Sisera the Canaanite; Barak ("Lightning"); the prophetess Devora Eshet Lapidot ("Torches")
51. Rachav's in the city of Jericho; the two Jewish spies sent by Yehoshua; not to kill Rachav's family when the Jews enter the city
52. Shaul, first King of Israel
53. the Jews; the Egyptians; the 9th plague of Darkness
54. the alphabet — *alef beit*
55. the spider who saved King David
56. the chariot which took the prophet Eliyahu Hanavi to heaven; Eliyahu
57. the Mearat Hamachpela in the city of Chevron
58. the Sanhedrin (High Court)
59. Yaakov and the angel
60. the Valley of Ayalon; the Jews and the Philistines

If you enjoyed TWISTERS, TEASERS, STUMPERS, send us some of your favorite Torah-teasing riddles. Or make some new ones up by yourself! If they are printed in another riddlebook, we'll mention your name and send you a free copy of the book. Send your stumpers to:

Yaffa Ganz c/o Feldheim Publishers POB 6525 Jerusalem, Israel